RABIES

RABIES

Lorrie Klosterman

 **Marshall Cavendish**
Benchmark
New York

Marshall Cavendish Benchmark
99 White Plains Road
Tarrytown, New York 10591-9001
www.marshallcavendish.us

This book is not intended for use as a substitute for advice, consultation, or treatment by a licensed medical
practitioner. The reader is advised that no action of a medical nature should be taken without consultation with a
licensed medical practitioner, including action that may seem to be indicated by the contents of this work, since
individual circumstances vary and medical standards, knowledge, and practices change with time. The publisher,
author, and medical consultants disclaim all liability and cannot be held responsible for any problems that may
arise from use of this book.

Library of Congress Cataloging-in-Publication Data

Klosterman, Lorrie.
  Rabies / by Lorrie Klosterman.
     p. cm. -- (Health alert)
  Summary: "Discusses rabies and its effects on people and
society"--Provided by publisher.
  Includes bibliographical references and index.
  ISBN 978-0-7614-2704-9
  1. Rabies--Juvenile literature. I. Title. II. Series.

  RC148.K56 2008
  616.9'53--dc22

2007008788

Front cover: Rabies viruses
Title page: Rabies viruses

Photo research by Candlepants Incorporated
Front cover: Eye of Science / Photo Researchers, Inc.
The photographs in this book are used by permission and through the courtesy of: *Photo Researchers, Inc.*: CMEABG-
UCBL-JOURBERT, 5; Chris Bjornberg, 12; Gerald C. Kelley, 13; Steve Maslowski, 14; Biophoto Associates, 16; Mehau
Kulyk, 19; AIRELLE-JOUBERT, 20; Dr. Gopal Murti, 22; Eye of Science, 25; Mary Evans, 31; Scott Camazine, 44; Lea
Paterson, 46. *The Image Works:* Science Museum/SSPL, 29; Mary Evans Picture Library, 32; SSPL, 39; Peter Hvizdak, 52;
Jim West, 54. *Shutterstock:* Cindy Haggerty, 40; Daniel Doubrovkine, 42; Jim Parkin, 50. *Corbis:* Bettmann, 35; Jessie
Cohen/Smithsonian, 55; Karen Kasmauski, 56. *Visuals Unlimited:* Dr. F.A. Murphy, 3, 11. *AP Photo:* Johnny Hanson, 17;
Morry Gash, 48. *LookatSciences/Phototake USA:* 57.

Printed in China
6 5 4 3 2 1

CONTENTS

1

WHAT IS IT LIKE TO HAVE RABIES?

When Lynne was nine, she and her brother, Bill, were visiting their grandparents in the countryside, as they often did. The two children always enjoyed walking down to the far end of the wheat field, to an old one-room school-house that no one used anymore. The paint was coming off and the windows were boarded up. The back door was open, which was how Lynne and Bill snuck inside. The schoolhouse was empty except for a few broken chairs covered in dust. The children liked to sit in the old schoolhouse and pretend they were teaching a class of ghosts.

One day, Lynne saw a tiny furry animal huddled on a windowsill. It looked like a dark brown mouse. Lynne loved animals and even had a pet mouse at home that she often held. She carefully scooped up the little creature to show her brother. Bill warned her that it was not a good idea to pick up wild animals, no matter how cute they were. Then he noticed it was a bat. The children could not resist gently opening one of its remarkable wings. When they did, the bat bit Lynne on the finger. She jumped and the animal fell to the ground. It did not get up, and stayed on the ground, weakly flapping its wings. Bill and Lynne decided to go home and wash their hands.

Lynne carefully washed her finger with soap and warm water. She did not want to tell her parents about it because she knew that she and Bill would get into trouble for going to the old schoolhouse. Lynne was not very worried about the bite because she could barely even see the tiny little teeth marks. But Bill remembered reading about rabies—a dangerous disease that animals can pass on to people. He told Lynne that bats could carry this deadly disease. Lynne and Bill decided that they needed to tell their parents about the bat bite.

Right away, their mother called the doctor and explained what had happened, while Bill took their father to the school to see if they could find the bat. The bat was right where it had fallen and it looked like it was dead. Bill's dad called the town's animal control officer who handled wild and stray animals. The animal control officer said that the bat looked like it was probably sick from rabies, and that other bats with rabies had been found in the area. He took the bat to be tested for rabies. It would take a few days before they got any test results.

Lynne's doctor did not want to wait to for the bat's test results, so he told the family to take Lynne to a hospital. The doctors at the hospital felt that Lynne should receive treatments to protect her just in case the bat had rabies. The doctors gave Lynne an injection, or shot, of medication in the finger with the bat bite. When she returned home, Lynne had five more shots in her arm over the next few weeks. Fortunately, Lynne did not have any problems after the treatments.

After the incident with the bat, Lynne decided to learn more about rabies. That was when she realized how danger-ous it can be to pick up a wild mammal—even one as cute as a shy little bat. She also read about a girl her age who had been bitten by a bat and died from rabies. No one had told a doctor about the bat bite until the girl began to get very sick. Unfortunately, by then it was too late for the treatments to help her. Lynne thanked her brother for convincing her to tell their parents about the bat bite.

Today, Lynne and Bill still like to take walks outside to enjoy nature. But they now know more about being safe when it comes to wild animals and the diseases they may carry.

2

WHAT IS RABIES?

Rabies is a serious illness caused by a **virus.** A virus is a tiny organism that gets inside a body and makes a person sick. The rabies virus invades the **nervous system,** especially the brain, and makes many more viruses. These viruses spread throughout the body, causing more illness. Without medical treatment to stop the spread of the viruses, rabies is always deadly. Fortunately, when it is caught in time, rabies is curable.

The type of virus that causes rabies makes certain animals sick, too. In fact, the disease is much more common in animals than it is in people. Still, rabies kills thousands of people worldwide each year. The World Health Organization (WHO), which keeps track of diseases around the globe, estimated in 2004 that 55,000 people die each year of rabies, mostly in

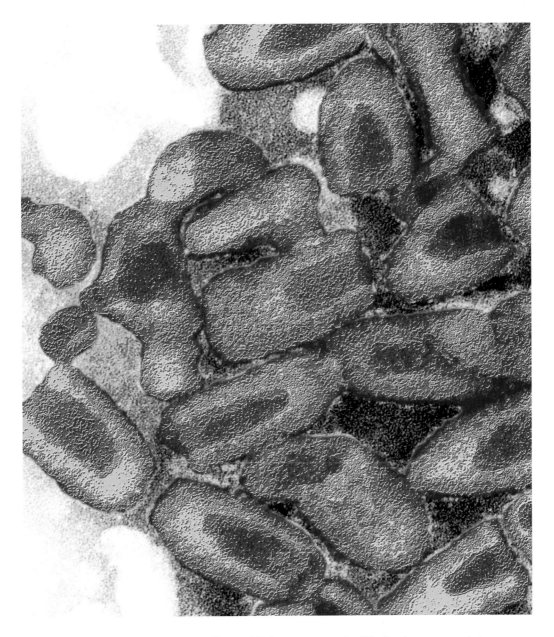

Rabies viruses are shaped like bullets. This image was magnified using a very strong microscope.

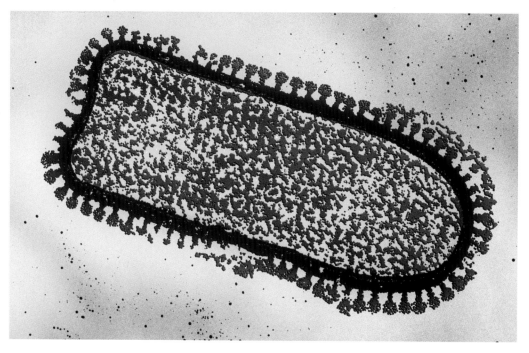

Rabies viruses can easily attach to cells, invading and infecting them and then spreading the disease.

poor areas of Africa and Asia where medical care can be hard to find. The WHO also estimates that about ten million people are treated for rabies each year.

In the United States, rabies has been reported in animals in every state except Hawaii. But human cases are not very common. For example, in 2004 there were only eight known human deaths due to rabies. During the ten years from 1990 to 2000, there were about three dozen rabies deaths in the United States. In the United States, more than one billion dollars is spent each year to help prevent, control, and treat rabies in animals and people.

THE ANIMAL CONNECTION

Almost everyone who has ever been infected with rabies caught it from an animal that had rabies, not from another person. In the United States, the ani-

Skunks are wild animals that can carry and spread rabies.

mal that passes rabies to humans is most often a bat. The other rabies cases are due to bites from other wild animals or from animals that are kept as pets, such as dogs and cats. In other countries, stray dogs are the most common animals to give rabies to people.

The rabies virus travels from animal to human through the animal's **saliva,** or spit. An animal infected with rabies has the virus in its saliva. When the animal bites a human, the

Many wild animals, such as raccoons, are drawn to the food in people's garbage. It is not uncommon for some homeowners to wake up in the middle of the night because a raccoon has knocked over a garbage can.

saliva enters the person's body. Rabies can also be passed along when an infected animal scratches a person. This happens if the animal has fresh saliva on its claws or feet. The rabies virus can also get into a person if the animal's saliva comes into contact with moist areas of a person's body, such as the eyes, mouth, or nose.

Some people become sick with rabies without knowing how they caught it. Medical researchers think that bats may be to blame for those cases. Bats can sometimes make their way into a house at night and then bite someone who is sleeping. The bites are often very small, and many people do not even realize they were bitten.

There are a few unfortunate instances in which a person has gotten rabies after receiving an organ transplant, such as a cornea, which is the clear surface of the eye. This can happen if the person who gave the organ was infected by rabies without knowing it. However, most organs are tested carefully to be sure the do not carry viruses.

Mammals and Rabies

Mammals are animals that have furry bodies, give birth to live babies, and produce milk for their young. Dogs, cats, bats, raccoons, and squirrels are mammals. Humans are mammals, though they are less furry than others! Only mammals can get sick with rabies because the rabies virus can only survive in mammals. Animals that are not mammals, such as birds, snakes, frogs, or fish, cannot get rabies.

Rabies is much more common in wild animals than in domesticated ones. This is because the rabies virus "hides out" in populations of wild mammals, where it is passed among a few of them year after year. Wild mammals that most often get rabies are raccoons, skunks, and bats. But foxes, coyotes, and less common mammals also can become sickened by the virus. They also can pass it when they bite or scratch another mammal.

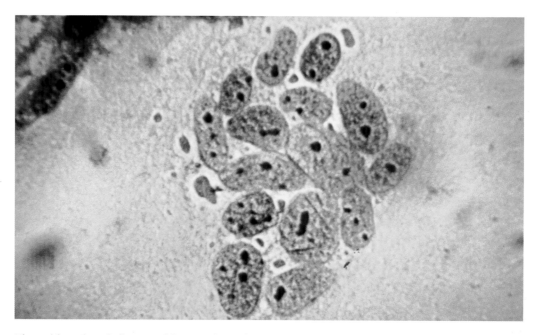

The rabies virus infects and harms the spinal cord and brain. This cell sample was taken from the brain of a dog that died from rabies.

With the exception of bats, it is rare to find a small mammal, such a mouse or squirrel, that has rabies. One reason for this is that a small animal that gets bitten by a rabies-infected animal will most likely be killed by the strength of the bite. If the small animal is dead, it does not have the chance to run around, passing along the virus to others. According to the U.S. Centers for Disease Control, small rodents, such as squirrels, rats, mice, hamsters, guinea pigs, gerbils, and chipmunks, are almost never found to be infected with rabies. They have not, so far, been known to cause rabies among humans in the

United States. Raccoons and skunks, on the other hand, are much larger and easy to see. They often wander out in the open when they have rabies.

Bats, though, are among the smallest of mammals but are a common carrier of rabies. Different types of bats carry slightly different types of rabies viruses. They pass the viruses around among members of their bat colonies, in the same way that illnesses are passed among people who live, work, or go to school together.

Researchers around the world study animals that can carry and spread rabies. By capturing and then examining mammals, such as bats, scientists hope to find a way to prevent and cure rabies.

Very few people will ever come across a **rabid** animal even though almost everyone has heard about the illness. In fact, some people are frightened to even see a raccoon, skunk, or bat, since they know these animals can carry rabies. An animal that is infected with rabies will behave strangely. For example, raccoons are usually only out at night, but a rabid raccoon might be wandering around a populated neighborhood during the day. An animal with rabies might be staggering or walking funny and it might be drooling a lot. Animals with rabies may also be aggressive, or likely to attack. Usually, most healthy mammals would sooner run away than face a human.

There are a few stories of a wild animal, such as raccoon or fox, wandering into a populated area and then chasing and biting someone. These stories are extremely rare and sometimes exaggerated. Regardless, everyone needs to be cautious around wild animals—and around domesticated ones—if the animals are behaving strangely or seem sick.

WHY IS RABIES SO DANGEROUS?

Brain Damage

The rabies virus causes a type of illness called **encephalitis.** Encephalitis means **inflammation,** or swelling, of the brain (*enceph-* refers to the brain, and *-itis* refers to inflammation).

The swelling happens because the brain is injured by the viruses. Viruses are able to get inside brain cells and make many, many copies of themselves. Eventually the infected cells die, damaging the brain. The viruses also spread to other cells and injure them, too.

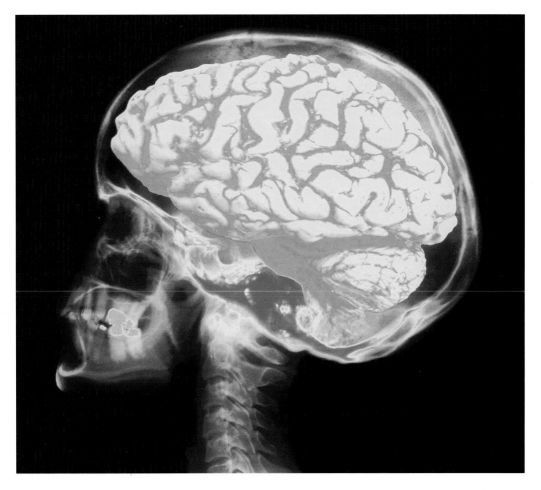

The hard bones of the skull and spine help to protect the delicate tissues and organs of the nervous system.

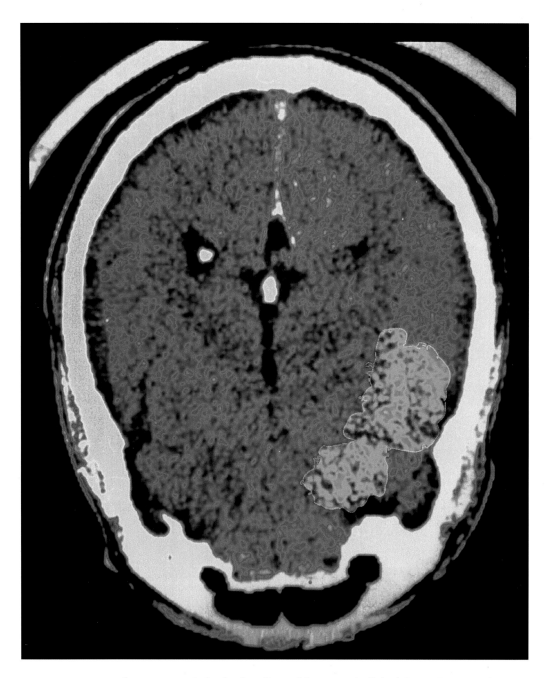

A computer scan shows parts of the brain affected by encephalitis (shown in orange).
Eventually, the swollen brain tissue will press against the skull, causing brain damage.

The Immune System Responds

The body's own reaction to the viruses also causes serious problems. Humans have a body system called the immune system. This system is made up of different organs, cells, and body fluids that work together to prevent and fight illness and disease. A special group of cells, called **white blood cells,** are part of the immune system. When a person becomes infected with a virus, his or her body directs white blood cells to gather at the area where the viruses are.

The white blood cells do their best to get rid of the viruses, and to clean away cells that have been injured or killed. With many viral illnesses, the body's immune system eventually "wins" the fight against viruses by destroying all of them. As they do this, the white blood cells release chemicals that attract watery fluid from the bloodstream. That fluid has healing substances in it, but it also causes swelling in the area where the viruses are. That is a serious problem when the viruses are in the brain. As the brain swells, there is no place for it to expand. This is because the brain is tightly held by bones of the skull. As a result, pressure builds up inside the skull as the bones push against the brain. That pressure

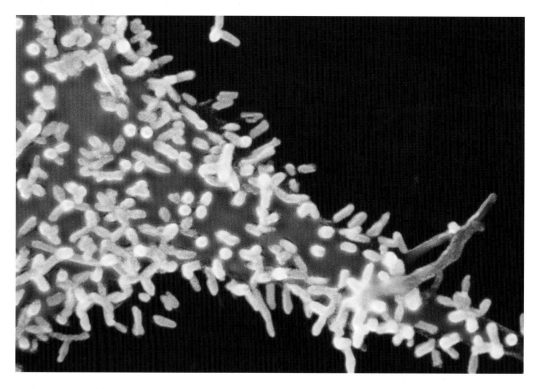

This magnified image shows rabies viruses attacking a cell inside the body. The small yellow structures are the rabies viruses, which are covering and invading the cell. Once they enter the cell, they will multiply and spread to other cells.

can quickly injure and even kill brain cells, which makes the person very ill.

Many illnesses besides rabies are caused by viruses, but people recover just fine most of the time. Common colds are caused by viruses, yet many people get better within weeks. So why is rabies deadly? Part of the reason is because infected brain cells are involved. Most viruses that people commonly catch do not do much harm to the brain.

MYTHS ABOUT RABIES

The best protection against rabies is knowing the facts—and myths—about the illness and the animals that carry it.

MYTH: You can get rabies by just touching an animal.
FACT: You cannot get rabies by simply petting an animal, or from touching the animal's blood, urine, or feces. Still, washing your hands after touching *any* animal—sick or healthy—is always a good idea.

MYTH: A family pet, such as a cat or dog, cannot give you rabies if it is friendly and does not bite or scratch.
FACT: Even domesticated animals that are friendly pets can catch and carry rabies. Always use caution whenever petting any animal. Always check with the owner before handling a pet.

MYTH: Rabies treatments that are given early are more painful than the disease itself.
FACT: Rabies treatments used to be very unpleasant, but that has changed. Today, the typical treatment for rabies is a series of shots, given on the arm, over a few weeks.

Rabies viruses are also deadly because they spread quickly through other parts of the nervous system—especially through nerves. Nerves are groups of living cells called **neurons.** Neurons within a nerve are very long and narrow, like extremely thin threads. Neurons carry special messages to and from the brain and **spinal cord.** (The spinal cord is an important collection of neurons that are enclosed within the backbone. The spinal cord is also connected to the brain.) The messages sent through nerves tell the brain what the body is feeling or what is happening to it. The brain and spinal cord then send messages through the nerves that will make the body respond in certain ways. Neurons are present everywhere in the body, making up a whole network of nerves. There are many just beneath the skin, where an animal could bite or scratch.

Rabies viruses are able to get into neurons at the bite area and travel to the spinal cord. From there they can travel through other neurons that go to the brain. The neurons are like a secret passageway the viruses follow throughout the nervous system. By doing this, many of the viruses are able to avoid white blood cells and other "soldiers" of the immune system. Over a period of several

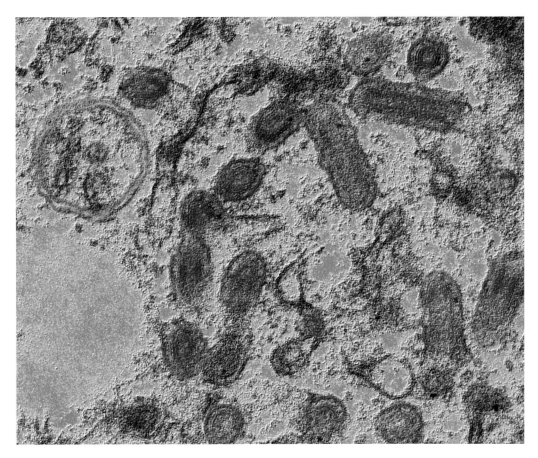

In an infected animal or human, the rabies viruses enter cells and damage them. This will interfere with normal body functions, causing illness and death.

weeks, the viruses multiply inside nerves and spread to the spinal cord and brain. By the time the immune system really notices the viruses and gets to work destroying them, it is too late. The immune system cannot get rid of the viruses fast enough. The viruses continue to multiply and destroy cells.

RABIES SYMPTOMS

As the rabies viruses invade the nervous system, symptoms of the illness will start to appear. Symptoms are changes in a person's body that make it obvious the person is sick. Symptoms of rabies can take a few weeks, or sometimes many weeks, to appear.

At first, symptoms are mild and are similar to those of some other common illnesses such as the flu. These symptoms include weakness, sleepiness, headache, fever, nausea, stiff muscles, and loss of appetite. Also, the area of the bite may become painful, itchy, or tingly. A person who has been exposed to the rabies virus but does not know it will probably think the problem is just a bad case of the flu.

However, after a few weeks, rabies viruses become more plentiful in the body. As a result, more serious symptoms start to show up. The person may become confused, unable to sleep, very anxious, and have hallucinations or imagine sights and sounds. Nerves throughout the body, not just in the brain, become damaged, too. Since nerves are responsible for physical sensations in your body, such as pain or itchiness, damage to nerves can trigger intense pain in the arms, legs, chest, or other parts of the body.

When the nerves are damaged, muscles cannot be controlled well. Walking or other normal activities that require movement become impossible. Muscles that control a person's breathing weaken. Muscles that control swallowing do not work well either, which may explain why many people who are sick with rabies do not want to drink anything and why animals with rabies drool a lot. Paralysis, which is the inability to move, can set in. The person may go into a **coma,** which is like a very deep sleep from which the person cannot be awakened.

Once these symptoms begin, even good medical care cannot save the person's life. This is why it is very important to understand how a person can be exposed to rabies. If it cannot be prevented completely, then at least there is a chance to get early treatment before symptoms appear.

3

THE HISTORY OF RABIES

Today we know that rabies is caused by a virus that invades the nervous system. But for centuries rabies was a mysterious and frightening illness. No one knew what caused it. Some of the earliest civilizations—ancient Rome, Greece, and Babylon—wrote about animals that behaved in strange ways. Those descriptions match a modern-day description of an animal with rabies. The disease has been around for a very long time.

Historians think that in ancient times animals that lived in North, Central, and South America did not carry the rabies virus. One idea about how the virus found its way to these continents is with colonists. The colonists transported farm animals and pets across the Atlantic Ocean on their ships. Infected animals may have been among them. These animals then infected the wild animals in the Americas.

Early scientists did not know about viruses or what caused rabies. Instead, they believed that most illnesses were spiritual or religious problems. As treatment, they suggested that sick people carry special items like this cloth talisman. This was supposed to cure the rabies and prevent more illness.

Over the centuries since then, the virus has spread from creature to creature in the North, Central, and South America. Today, there are several forms, or strains, of the virus, and rabies viruses have spread to almost all regions of the world. Bats, which can fly long distances and even migrate between continents just as people do, probably have spread the viruses around.

FINDING THE INVISIBLE

For many years, anyone who was infected with rabies always died. Doctors and scientists knew that rabies was a deadly disease. But they did not have special microscopes that could see objects as tiny as a virus. So they did not know exactly what caused rabies or how it could be treated.

A treatment for rabies was discovered as an experiment during a desperate situation. In 1885 Joseph Meister, a nine-year-old boy living in Germany, was bitten by a rabid dog. His parents hoped they could get help from Louis Pasteur, a French scientist who had made many remarkable discoveries having to do with **microorganisms.** Fortunately, Joseph's parents went to the right man for help. Pasteur and other researchers had been experimenting for years to find treatments that could save rabbits and dogs

Louis Pasteur was famous for discovering a treatment for rabies. He is also credited with developing pasteurization, which is a process that kills harmful germs in food and beverages.

from dying of rabies. They had found that bits of ground up spinal cord from a rabid animal could actually help protect another animal from dying of rabies. The spinal cord material was treated first with heating, and then injected into the animal.

It was a big decision to inject Joseph with the spinal cord material. It had never been done with a person. However, Pasteur and Joseph's parents felt that it was their only option. Fortunately, it worked and Joseph survived.

Today we know that spinal cord bits from animals infected with rabies contain a lot of rabies viruses. The heating process inactivates the virus, which means the viruses are less dangerous and will not cause the disease. But they still can cause an animal's or person's body to think the virus is attacking them. That triggers disease-fighting cells of the immune system. The immune cells act as though they are fighting off the disease. These immune cells remain activated for some

LES GRANDS MAUX ET LES GRANDS REMÈDES 161

Base du cerveau, nerf optique et nerf ophthalmique
Mélancolie Hallucinations.

Nerfs hypoglosse et glosso-pharyngien.
Constrictions de la gorge. Hydrophobie

Nerf récurrent ou laryngé inférieur.
Étranglement.
Spasme de la glotte.

Plexus pulmonaire du nerf pneumogastrique.
Suffocations Étouffement.

Cerveau.

Bulbe du cerveau.
Siége central de l'irritation rabique.

Cervelet.

Filets gastriques terminaux du nerf pneumogastrique.

Mécanisme des principaux accidents déterminés.par le virus de la rage.

Published in a French medical book from the late 1800s, this illustration shows the organs affected by the rabies virus.

time, and are able to fight off the real viruses if the animal or person is exposed to them later.

That success was the beginning of rabies treatments—something that was needed worldwide. By 1890, the Pasteur rabies **immunization** was saving lives of many people around the

VACCINATIONS

An immunization or vaccination is a shot that a person gets in order to be protected from diseases. Often, vaccinations are given even if the person is not expected to come into contact with the disease-causing microorganism. For example, children in the United States get many immunizations when they are very young. The vaccinations are supposed to prevent illnesses, such as rubella or measles, even though most American children will not be exposed to those diseases. There are also vaccines for common illnesses like the flu or chicken-pox. Usually, these vaccines are not dangerous and do more good than harm.

Since the rabies vaccine can cause problems, it is only given if a person has been exposed to rabies. But people who are traveling to areas of the world where rabies is a more common problem may want to get the vaccination before they go. People who often work with wild animals that get rabies may want to get a rabies vaccination.

globe. This treatment was called an immunization because it triggered an immune response that protects against the disease. The treatment can also be called a **vaccination,** since the person is being injected with a vaccine made up of inactive viruses.

In the years that followed Pasteur's discovery, the treatments for people who were bitten by a rabid animal improved. But even as late as the 1950s, the rabies immunization shots were injected into the abdomen, or stomach area. This was very painful, and it took nearly two dozen shots to be sure the person was protected! Also, the spinal cord material from animals sometimes made people very sick. That is because some people's immune systems had such a strong reaction to this "foreign" animal material that they died. Another downside of the vaccine was that it contained formaldehyde, a chemical that is very poisonous. Because of these problems, the immunizations were given only to people who might already have been exposed to rabies. Sometimes the treatments did not work.

RABIES TREATMENTS TODAY

Pasteur's immunization is still used to treat people today, though the method has changed a bit. For example, there are fewer shots, and they are injected into the muscles of the arm.

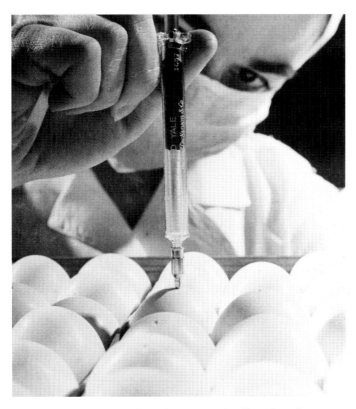

Some vaccines are made using eggs. The live virus is injected into a chick embryo (a developing chicken) inside an egg. The virus makes millions of copies of itself in the egg. The viruses are then harvested and used to make vaccines.

Other types of rabies vaccinations have also been created. One that works even better and is safer is made using cells in culture. This means the cells used in the vaccine are not in an animal any-more, but instead are kept in a nutri-ent liquid called a culture. The cells can live in this cul-ture for many years, making parts of the viruses that are used in the vaccine. Additionally, **antibodies,** or **immunoglobulins,** are given to the patient. These antibodies are immunity material that was made by animals that were exposed to the rabies viruses. The hope is that the animals' antibodies will help a person's immune system fight rabies.

Even though rabies treatments work well for most people, tens of thousands of people still die of rabies each year. Many people do not know how to spot a rabid animal, so they do not take the proper steps to keep safe. If they are infected by the rabid animal, most do not know that they must seek medical help immediately.

Another reason why people die from rabies is because the shots are not easy to deliver to people who live in villages out in the countryside. This is where rabies is often a very big problem. Many people in Southeast Asia and China, for example, are far away from doctors and medical facilities. The treatments are also very expensive—they cost anywhere from a thousand to several thousand dollars a person! People who have medical insurance or enough money can afford the vaccine, but many more cannot.

Fortunately, governments around the world are getting serious about vaccinating and controlling animals that spread the disease. Laws in the United States require rabies vaccinations for all cats and dogs that are kept as pets. Animal control services take extra precautions to control rabid animals in the wild. Many governments and health organizations are also working to make the treatments easier to get, and less expensive.

RABIES EPIDEMICS

Animals sometimes have epidemics of rabies. An epidemic is when many cases of a disease show up in a small geographical area at the same time. For example, the northeastern United States has had many cases of rabies among raccoons and skunks in the past several years.

In other areas of the world, epidemics among dogs are sometimes a serious problem because the dogs are not protected from the disease. For example, on Flores Island in Indonesia there had not been any rabies among their dogs until three sick dogs were brought there in 1997. Over the next five years, thousands of dogs became infected with rabies, and over one hundred people died from rabies-infected dog bites. Hundreds of thousands of dogs have been killed there in an effort to control the epidemic. On the island today, there are fewer cases of people dying from rabies because they are getting proper medical treatment.

4

PREVENTING, DIAGNOSING, AND TREATING RABIES

The best way to prevent getting sick from rabies is to be safe and avoid any chance of coming into contact with a rabid animal. This means being careful when walking in wooded or wild areas and not touching any wild animals. Using caution around pets that are not familiar to you is also a good idea. But if you do come into contact with a rabid animal, there are important steps you must take.

Medical treatment for rabies is essential to save a person's life. Treatment for rabies must start before symptoms show up. That is unusual. For most illnesses, a doctor will treat a person only *after* symptoms appear. The symptoms are how the doctor—and the patient—know something is wrong. But with rabies, waiting until symptoms appear

Ministry of Agriculture
Fisheries and Food

YOU ARE ENTERING AN INFECTED AREA

RABIES

If an area is suspected of having large populations of animals with rabies, warning signs may be posted. This could prevent people from coming into contact with the rabid animals.

is too late. The body's immune system cannot fight off the virus quickly enough on its own. The immune system needs help to win its battle against the rabies virus.

WHEN TO CALL A DOCTOR

If a person does not have symptoms of rabies, how does she or he know to get rabies treatment? There are some very important clues that everyone should be aware of. If a child or teenager is bitten or scratched by any animal, an adult needs to be told. A parent, guardian, or another adult will help with the next steps.

Anyone who is bitten by a mammal, whether a wild one or a pet, must think of rabies as a possibility. A scratch from an animal, too, might transfer the virus. Treatment begins right away by washing the injured area very well with soap and water for about five minutes. A good washing is important for any bite or scratch, even if rabies is not a possibility. A **germ**-killing liquid or spray should be applied, too.

Handwashing is a good way to avoid catching many illnesses, including rabies. But other steps are needed to prevent getting sick with rabies.

An important question will help decide what to do next: Is the animal wild or domesticated and kept as a pet or farm animal? If it is a wild animal, such as a bat, raccoon, or skunk, a doctor must be contacted immediately or the person must go to a hospital's emergency room. Doctors will ask about the behavior of the animal to find clues about its chances of carrying the disease. To be safe, however, rabies treatment will probably be started right away. If the animal is not wild, but is a stray dog, cat, or other stray pet, it must be treated like a wild animal. No one really knows the history of a stray pet. So a doctor must be called immediately.

If the animal is obviously someone's pet, important information is needed. First, does the animal have an up-to-date rabies vaccination? All pet owners of dogs, cats, and ferrets are supposed to keep their pets vaccinated against rabies. If the animal that bit or scratched someone is vaccinated against rabies, it should be kept away from people and watched closely for ten days. This is to see if it has symptoms of rabies anyway, just in case the animal's rabies vaccination is not working, which sometimes happens.

If there is no information about rabies vaccination, or if the owner has not kept the pet vaccinated, rabies is a serious possibility. The only way to tell for sure if an animal is infected

Pets that have been vaccinated against rabies should have identification tags on their collars. These tags will tell animal control that the animal is safe, and may prevent unnecessary killing of lost pets.

with the rabies virus is to kill it and have an animal doctor examine its brain for signs of **infection.** Sometimes when a pet bites a person it must be killed to figure this out. Pet owners can prevent this sad fate by keeping their animal's vaccinations current. Special tags for a pet's collar are given out by veterinarians who give the vaccine so that the animal carries proof of its vaccination.

EARLY TREATMENT

The treatment a person gets before showing signs of rabies is called **PEP.** That is short for postexposure prophylaxis. "Postexposure" means that the treatment starts after a person has been around the rabies virus. "Prophylaxis" refers to something that is given as a prevention. For rabies, PEP prevents the virus from spreading and making the person ill.

PEP is a series of shots that contain antibodies. These are microscopic particles made by cells of the immune system. *Anti-* means "against." Antibodies work against invaders— viruses, bacteria, and other disease-causing microorganisms. Antibodies stick to the surfaces of the invaders and make it easier for the body to notice them and destroy them. They are like a handle that immune cells can grab onto so they can then break apart the invader. Antibodies are also called immunoglobulins, meaning they are large proteins (globulins) of the immune system.

The antibodies in the rabies shots are usually from horses. The horses were given a small amount of weakened virus that

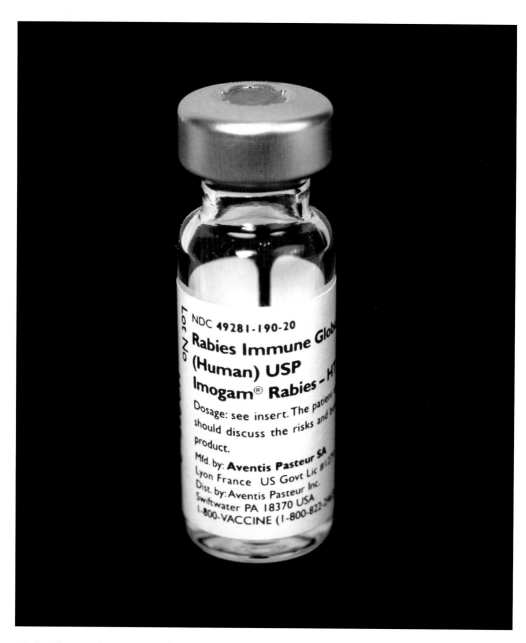

If the disease is caught early, there are a number of treatments that can be used to help infected people, including rabies immunoglobulins.

would not kill them, but caused them to make antibodies to fight the virus. The antibodies are then taken out of the animal's blood in small amounts and made as pure as possible. Then the antibodies are frozen and kept in hospitals, where they can be quickly thawed and given in shots to humans.

The first rabies shot is given near the bite area, to help fight viruses that might be present there. Over the next few weeks, five more injections are given to wipe out the viruses wherever they may have spread. Sometimes the antibodies in the shots can make a person very sick. But with good medical care, the person can handle the sickness and survive the rabies.

If someone has been bitten by an animal that might have rabies, other people who were around them at the time might need to get treated. This is because there might be a chance that they also came into contact with the animal's saliva. If someone has started to have rabies symptoms, it is even more important to treat other people besides the patient. This is because the virus particles will be in the patient's saliva, and might have been transferred to friends or family by sharing beverages or foods. In addition, doctors and nurses who have been in contact with the person might take the rabies treatments as well, just to be safe. There have not

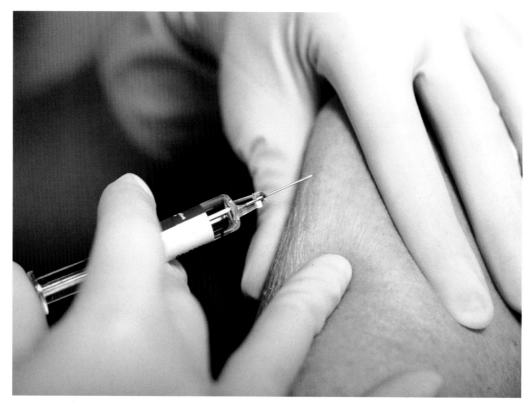

Vaccinations for many different diseases are recommended in order for a person to stay healthy. Some vaccinations are even required by law.

actually been any cases of a doctor or nurse getting rabies from a patient, though, because they already are very careful to protect themselves as they work.

TREATMENT AFTER SYMPTOMS APPEAR

For people who start to get sick with rabies, doctors will do several things. One is to give the patient a rabies vaccine.

The vaccine contains small amounts of weakened virus that do not cause illness. Instead, the weakened viruses are like a loud wake-up call to the immune system, telling it to become more active in its efforts to wipe out the virus.

Doctors will also inject antibodies into the person's bloodstream. Those antibodies help the immune system destroy the virus. Special drugs are also given. Some of them, such as ribavirin, help to stop the viruses from making more copies of themselves. These are called **antiviral drugs.** If such drugs could stop every last virus from doing that, the person would have a greater chance of recovering from the illness. But some of the viruses can escape the drugs' effects.

Another substance, called interferon (named after the word *interfere*) may help, too. The body makes interferon when its cells are invaded by viruses. The interferon helps boost the activities of immune cells. Interferon is given to rabies patients in the hopes it will improve the patient's chances of beating the infection.

Even with those treatments—vaccines, antibodies, antiviral drugs, and interferon—there is only one known case in the United States of someone surviving rabies after symptoms started. That person, a fifteen-year-old girl, had another treatment as well. Her doctors gave her drugs to put her into

Jeanne Giese was the only person who survived a rabies infection wihtout receiving the vaccine. She contracted rabies when she was bitten by a bat in her church. A medically induced coma and other treatments helped her to get better. She still has some health issues, but is on the road to recovery.

a coma. A coma is like a very deep sleep. Nothing can awaken a person in a coma because the body's activities become very slow. Even the brain, which is quite active during sleep, is deeply resting during a coma. When doctors use drugs to put the patient in a coma, it is said to be "medically induced." (Comas can also occur when a person is in an accident or has some injury to the brain.) For a medically induced coma, drugs are given until there is hope that the person has fought the illness well enough to recover. Then the drugs are stopped, their effects wear off, and the person awakens.

It is not certain just how the coma may have helped fight the rabies viruses. One idea, though, is that the girl's body was able to rest deeply, so it could use most of its energy to fight the virus. During that time, virus-killing medicines had time to help her immune system, too. However, even with the treatments and the coma, the girl still has health problems to overcome.

PREVENTION

Because rabies can be deadly even with treatments, it is important for people to prevent their exposure to the virus. Everyone can take steps to prevent rabies. Always use caution when walking in wooded areas or in regions where there are many wild mammals. You should never interfere with any wild animals, but there is no need to fear them in general. Many animals have been entering neighborhoods, yards, garages, and sheds because people's homes have spread into so many areas that used to be wild. Most of these animals are healthy.

However, you should never touch a wild animal no matter how cute or harmless it appears to be.

Always be on the lookout for mammals that look ill or are coming your way. One quick way to tell if an animal is sick with rabies is by figuring out if it is supposed to be out during the day. For example, raccoons mainly walk around at night. If you see one wobbling around during the day or huddled on a front porch in the middle of the day, chances are good that the animal is sick. Also, animals that are sick with rabies often will not run from people as they usually would. An animal with rabies might have trouble walking, it might be turning in circles, or it might fall down a lot. Rabid animals usually drool a lot, since they cannot swallow well. Of course, an animal that

Animal control officers are specially trained to handle cases in which animals may be infected with rabies.

has any of these behaviors might just be hurt or lost instead of having rabies.

Whatever the case may be, avoid these animals and call your local police or animal control officers. Animal control officers are trained to recognize rabid animals and to capture them. (They are also trained to catch wild or stray animals that are healthy.) The officer also will know if there is an epidemic of rabies in wild animal populations in the area.

If a pet is suspected of having rabies, it will be captured and taken away for observation for a few weeks to see if it develops rabies symptoms. If it does, it must be killed. A wild animal is often killed on the spot (usually with a gun) so no one is bitten or scratched while trying to capture it. Although it is sad to imagine this fate, a rabid animal is in bad shape and will die soon, after a lot of suffering and pain. Also, killing infected animals prevents them from infecting yet more wild animals, pets, or even people.

Rabies cannot be passed on from an object to a person— unless the object has fresh rabies-infected saliva on it. So you should not fear enjoying the outdoors and viewing wildlife from a safe distance. Always wash your hands well after you have been outdoors or after you have handled any animals. The simple act of hand washing can kill many germs lurking

Dogs and cats that are suspected of carrying rabies are quarantined and kept away from other animals and humans. If the animal shows no symptoms, it will usually be returned to its owner or placed in a good home. However, animals with rabies have to be put to sleep.

around on your hands. To get your hands really clean, doctors suggest using warm water and soap. When your hands are wet with soap and water, rub your hands together, making sure to clean between your fingers and under your fingernails. Many doctors recommend washing and rinsing your hands for at least thirty to forty seconds, or as long as it takes you to sing the *Alphabet Song*. Be sure to dry your hands on a clean towel or clean paper towels.

Prevention in Pets

It is very important that pet owners vaccinate their pets against rabies. There are vaccines for dogs, cats, ferrets, horses, cattle, and sheep. Rabies vaccinations do not last forever, so the pet needs to get vaccinated every few years. Veterinarians will remind owners to keep a pet's rabies vaccination up to date. Even indoor pets should be vaccinated if other pets visit them, or if bats get into the house, such as through an attic window. Some towns have rabies clinics in which people from all around the town can bring in their pets to be vaccinated, at low cost. Often the town officials or charities will organize this and help cover expenses for the hundreds of vaccinations that are given on a clinic day.

Another way to prevent rabies is to reduce the number of stray pets. Sometimes a pet owner just does not want the pet anymore, or cannot care for it. Abandoning the animal is not the answer. Instead, the right thing to do is to give the animal to a local humane society, shelter, or animal rescue group. The pet will be safe and cared for until a new owner is found. This is important because pets that become lost or are abandoned by their owners must roam outdoors looking for food and shelter. They are

Rabies clinics offer low-cost or free rabies vaccinations for cats and dogs. These clinics help to keep rabies cases low.

much more likely to cross paths with wild animals and catch diseases like rabies. Many people care about animals and work to help strays. There are organizations that will capture and care for stray pets, including vaccinating them, and finding them new homes.

Even mammals in zoos and nature parks are vaccinated against diseases like rabies.

VACCINATING IN THE WILD

Vaccines against rabies have been created by scientists so that wild animals, not just pets, can be vaccinated. Because there are several different types of the rabies virus, many vaccines have been developed. Some countries have brought rabies under control by putting the vaccine into food and dropping the food all over the countryside by airplane for wild and stray animals to eat.

However, wildlife vaccines have not worked well in skunks, one of the main rabies carriers in the United States. Bernhard Dietzschold, a veterinarian and professor of microbiology and immunology at Jefferson Medical College in Philadelphia, and his coworkers are just some of the scientists trying to find a way to prevent, fight, and defeat rabies. Dr. Dietzschold and his team have come up with a new vaccine that looks like it will work well and be safe in skunks as well as in many other animals. If so, rabies in skunks may soon be under better control.

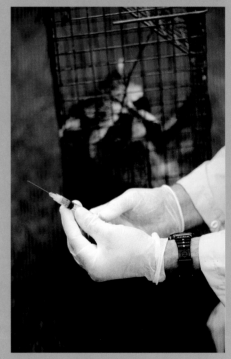

New vaccination programs designed to protect wild animals against rabies may help curb the spread of the disease to domesticated animals and humans.

Researchers continue to search for ways to control—and maybe someday eradicate— rabies.

People of all ages can help prevent rabies. All it takes is a little bit of knowledge about the disease and a kindness and respect for animals. Treating wild animals and pets properly and respecting their boundaries is one way to reduce your chances of getting rabies. Knowing how best to prevent the disease, and what steps need to be taken to treat it, can save your life.

GLOSSARY

antibodies—Small particles that help fight infection by sticking to microorganisms such as viruses and bacteria, making them easier for the immune system to destroy.

antiviral drug—A medicine that kills viruses and prevents them from making more copies of themselves.

coma—An unconscious state from which a person cannot be awakened.

encephalitis—An illness in which the brain is swollen, usually because viruses or bacteria have gotten into it and caused an infection.

epidemic—A situation in which many people or animals have the same kind of illness at the same time.

germ—A disease-causing microorganism, such as a virus or bacterium.

immune system—The body's group of white blood cells and antibodies (made by certain immune cells) which work together to destroy viruses, bacteria, and other things that can cause illness.

immunization—A preventive procedure in which harmless forms of a microorganism are injected into a person to make the immune system stronger.

immunoglobulins—Small particles that help fight infection by sticking to microorganisms such as viruses and bacteria, making them easier for the immune system to destroy. Also called antibodies.

infection—Having bacteria, viruses, parasites, or other organisms living in some part of the body and causing injury.

inflammation—The body's response to injury, which helps heal the injured area, but which can also harm the body by causing too much swelling and pressure.

microorganism—A virus, bacterium, or other tiny microscopic organism. Some cause human and animal diseases, but many are harmless.

nervous system—The brain, spinal cord, and network of nerves and neurons throughout the body.

neuron—A type of cell that carries messages to and from the brain and controls whatever the body is doing.

PEP—Stands for postexposure prophylaxis, which is the treatment given to someone who may have been exposed to the rabies virus.

rabid—Having rabies.

saliva—The moisture in an animal's or person's mouth; also known as spit.

spinal cord—A bundle of nerves running inside the backbone (spine) that connect the brain with the rest of the body.

symptoms—Changes in a person's body that make it obvious a person is sick.

vaccination—Giving a shot (or several) that has a weakened virus in it, which boosts the body's ability to fight that virus.

virus—One of the smallest things known to cause illnesses, and which must be inside a living creature because a virus cannot live on its own. There are many different kinds of viruses.

white blood cells—Cells that are part of the immune system and protect the body against infections.

FIND OUT MORE

Books

Alphin, Elaine Marie. G*erm Hunter: A Story about Louis Pasteur.* Minneapolis, MN: Carolrhoda Books, 2003.

Evans-Martin, F. Fay . *The Nervous System.* New York: Chelsea House, 2005.

Kienzle, Thomas E. *Rabies.* New York: Chelsea House, 2006.

Snedden, Robert. *Fighting Infectious Diseases.* Chicago: Heinemann Library, 2000.

Web Sites

Kids' Health: Rabies
http://kidshealth.org/kid/health_problems/infection/rabies.html

Neuroscience for Kids: Rabies
http://faculty.washington.edu/chudler/rabies.html

Centers for Disease Control: Rabies
http://www.cdc.gov/ncidod/dvrd/kidsrabies

American Veterinary Medical Association: What You Should Know about Rabies
http://www.avma.org/communications/brochures/rabies/rabies_
    brochure.asp

ABOUT THE AUTHOR

Lorrie Klosterman is a biologist and writer. She has written about many health topics for books and magazines. Lorrie loves wild animals and hopes that young people learn to respect and enjoy wild animals, too. She and her daughter and their pet cats adore the skunks, opossums, raccoons, bats, woodchucks, squirrels, foxes, and other mammals and birds that share the yard around their house. Some of the skunks, and a stray cat, have gotten rabies, so she keeps her pets vaccinated against rabies

INDEX